In the Eyes of a Dog

Also by Kevin Pilkington

Reading Stone, 1988
On This Quiet Hill, 1990
Getting By, 1996
Spare Change, 1997
St. Andrew's Head, 2003
Ready to Eat the Sky, 2004

In the Eyes of a Dog

Kevin Pilkington

The New York Quarterly Foundation, Inc.
New York, New York

NYQ Books™ is an imprint of The New York Quarterly Foundation, Inc.

The New York Quarterly Foundation, Inc.
P. O. Box 2015
Old Chelsea Station
New York, NY 10113

www.nyqbooks.org

Copyright © 2009 by Kevin Pikington

All rights reserved. No part of this book may be used or reproduced in any manner whatsoever without written permission of the author. This book is a work of fiction. Any references to historical events, real people or real locales are used fictitiously. Other names, characters, places, and incidents are products of the author's imagination, and any resemblance to actual events or locales or persons, living or dead, is entirely coincidental.

First Edition

Set in New Baskerville

Layout and Design by Raymond P. Hammond
Cover Illustration: © 2009 D Photo / IllustrationWorks

Library of Congress Control Number: 2009931018

ISBN: 978-1-935520-09-2

In the Eyes of a Dog

Acknowledgments

Some of the poems in this collection have appeared in various forms in the journals: *The New York Quarterly, The River Oak Review, Jelly Bucket, The Vermont Literary Review, The Cortland Review, The Valparaiso Review,* and in the chapbooks: *Reading Stone, Getting By* and *St. Andrew's Head.*

For the women who mean the most:

Lillian, Celia, Maureen and Sylvia

Contents

I. Crossing the River

Therapy	13
The River	14
Shopping	16
Making a Phone Call with the Moon	18
Extra Income	19
Poem with Mel Tormé's Voice	20
Train with Snow and Ice	22
Greatness Isn't Always the Color of Envy	24
Sunday Afternoon, 1:15pm	26
Eating a Herd of Reindeer	27
The City, the Snow and Two People Only	28
Butterfly	30
Shadow	31
Strong Coffee	32
Meteor Shower	34
An Act of Seduction in the Twenty-first Century	36
A Type of Love Story	37
Traffic in Your Chest	38
Smoke	40
Crossing the River	41

II. Homesick

Havana Burning	45
Mango	46
In the Eyes of a Dog	48
Kissing the Sky	50
Basketball	52
La Jolla	54
Camden	55
The Cavandish Firehouse Benefit Dance	56
Maggots	59
On the Harbor	60
Wellfleet	62
Hiking	64
House of Books	66
Tequila	68
Baja	70
Near the Lake	72
Capri	75
Homesick	78

I. Crossing the River

"There is no solitude in the world like that of the big city."

— Kathleen Norris

Therapy

Once it was easier to love
an entire country rather than just
one person. Then you met a girl
who chewed gum that snapped
in her mouth like tiny firecrackers.
Each day you spent with her
was the Fourth of July and the first
night you slept together was the only
time in your life you felt patriotic.

You spend too much time thinking
about the past, though sometimes
it can't be helped. When the weather
report said the temperature would
reach the 60s over the next few days,
it made you take out your old Beatles
albums and play them all week.

Therapy is helping you deal more
and accept what's going on around you
now. So when you see another magazine
with a member of the Royal Family
on the cover and get disgusted with all
the money wasted on them, you have
to remind yourself how you always
wanted to be the next King of Swing.

You are also learning to make peace
with the fact that when the doorbell
rings the poodle in the apartment
next door will always bark in French
instead of English. And how the car horns
in heavy traffic along First in rush hour
are beginning to sound more and more
like Gershwin everyday.

The River

I sit on a bench next to the river.
The streets are far enough away
so by the time the sound of traffic
reaches me it massages my back.
I've come here before to figure
things out or just read. Last week
it was a novel I got hooked on,
inhaling every sentence as if they
were lines of coke. Mostly it's just
to look at the river; the tide stays wet,
each wave soaked all the way
through—making it easier for ships
to enter and leave the harbor.
When a page from a newspaper
grabs my ankle like a small dog
I pick it up, crumble it into
a basketball and shoot it into a trash
bin a few feet away as thousands cheer.

I then look across the river past
its banks that in this section of the city
are filled with rock and concrete instead
of cash, to the road and parked cars
where drivers go to come for twenty bucks.
I can almost make out a hooker's head
bobbing up and down in the front seat
as if it were floating on waves.

Dark water keeps most gulls away,
though eagles fly low in a flock
of tattoos on men who work tankers
and tugs. I know enough not to stare
at the water too long since it will pollute
my eyes and turn them brown but it's the only
river I've got. The pigeons that land near
my feet are always gray from rubbing
against sky and when I stomp my foot,
I know they'll fly away full on plans
that never worked out for me.
Plans that become just so many crumbs
I bring to feed them in brown paper bags.

Shopping

An old man on the corner sells
white socks laid out on a table
like flounder in the Third Street
Fish Market. You pick out a size
nine, ask him to filet them so no bones
will get stuck in your feet.

You stop in the Army & Navy store
to buy a sweater, bright green,
but it's not as loud as the girl
in the apartment below yours
who screams God so often
when she fucks, you are beginning
to believe he really exists.

You stroll past the pawnshop
where a couple of months ago
you hocked ten years of your life
for one hundred bucks, ten more than you
expected. When you landed a job
you went back, saw them in the window
then went in and bought the guitar
they were next to instead.

On the next corner, the tall guy
from Ghana is back selling
watches from his briefcase.
You buy one every few weeks
after it breaks down but like the way
they run fast, making work days
go by so quickly Friday begins on Thursday.

Before going home you decided
to stop off and see the woman
you've been going out with
for the past month. You want
to apologize for last night's argument
but if she asks one more time
who you are trying to fool
you can hold up your wrist, point
to your Rolex and say, nobody but myself.

Making a Phone Call with the Moon

The new high rise going up across the street
is the same one I walked past last weekend.
It has twenty more stories although none look
worth reading. They tore down the old tenements
that stood there for years with the kind of windows
Hopper looked in to paint women who sat in their slips
on the edge of beds and stared out into empty sky.

The name they will place over the doors is on
a temporary sign a cement truck is parked in front of.
I do remember there is an H in it that remains silent
whenever the construction stops. At the corner
when the traffic light makes me see red I stay calm,
don't get mad and just wait for it to change again,
pleased that I'm learning to control my anger
and walking in the right direction.

Two blocks up is the office building I found
myself in front of one night when I needed
to make a phone call. With no change in my pocket
and the moon the size of a quarter, I made my way
to the roof, reached up and peeled it off the sky.
Later I found a payphone, dropped it in and yelled
until I spit stars. Of course that must have happened before
I stopped drinking or perhaps it happened to someone
else. It just doesn't sound like something I would do,
it really doesn't.

Extra Income

Both sides of the street
are crowded with pedestrians
waiting for the lights to change.
An attractive woman across
the way stares in my direction,
so I inch closer to the curb
to get nearer to the heavy traffic
that always makes me look
thinner. A long line of cabs
creates a yellow spine, causing
First Avenue to look scared or
at least seem afraid to move uptown.

A jogger who pushes his way in front
of me should be wearing a t-shirt
to cover the hair on his back
that looks like smoke from hundreds
of tiny campfires his sweat
just put out.

Next to him an older woman
tells a friend she's on her way
to the beauty salon to have her hair
piled higher on her head since
she has been converting her curls
into apartments and renting them
out for extra income.

As the light changes and everyone
crosses, I hear her say she didn't
need so much space, that's why
last month she moved downstairs
into the small studio nearest
her skull.

Poem with Mel Tormé's Voice

Rain has moved out of the city
and left behind fog that looks
like Mel Tormé's voice covering
the top floors of a high rise.
A woman leaning against an office
building takes out a cigarette, lights it
then keeps her mouth open to let the smoke
slowly crawl out then travels up
past her eyes until her face resembles London.

Noise from traffic never stays
white as I walk between cars
to cross the street and avoid the guy
coming towards me. He lives down
the hall and feels he has to talk
although I always carry the conversation.
With a bad back, I thought it best
not to do any heavy lifting.

On Third I feel a shortness of breath
again. The doctor last week showed
me an x-ray of my lungs that looked
like two porterhouse steaks. He said
they were fine and it was nothing more
than nerves. It's just that I worry
he might be wrong. In a few minutes,
I feel fine again and with the sky clearing,
I make my way home.

I take the elevator to the roof, pleased
it's an express, stand there and look out
at the East River. I have a good view
of Queens, its lights are low
and glowing—charcoal perfect for grilling.
So I hurry down to my apartment,
come back with a can of beer,
pull the pin like it's a grenade,
throw a couple of burgers on Astoria
and listen to them sizzle.

Train with Snow and Ice

Snow fell last night
then turned on its side,
like a restless man trying to sleep,
into ice. This morning
the 10:05 train out of Grand
Central tries to shake us warmer.
The first stop is 128th Street
since it won't melt back
into 125th until the end of the week
when temperatures are expected
to rise.

The Bronx looks frozen stiff.
Buildings don't move,
trees are covered in glass
kids break with bricks
to steal bark and smoke
from factories turn cotton
in the cold.

I turn to catch a glimpse
of Manhattan that is a few inches
wide and the Empire State,
a syringe I would use if I weren't
already hooked on the city.
At Fordham the conductor
announces ice on the tracks
has forced this local into
an express that won't be able
to stop until North White Plains.

I lean my head back against
the seat, close my eyes
and begin falling asleep
at Fleetwood where the snow
begins falling again like sugar,
making a little girl holding
onto her mother's hand
look even sweeter.

Greatness Isn't Always the Color of Envy

William Butler Yeats lives across the street.
It's easy to spot him every morning heading
to the deli. He wears a big bowtie that resembles
a deflated balloon drooping down from his neck.

His puffy white hair looks like a cloud
needing a little gel and combed neatly against
the sky. I try to avoid him these days
though often bump into him as he walks back
to his apartment with a coffee in his hand
and the Irish Echo folded under his arm.

For the last month Virgil makes extra money
driving a tour bus. He wants me to hop on and tour
the downtown area—streets and buildings
I already know. It's a red double-decker
but I haven't returned his calls.

I try not to pass the Starbucks near Third
on my way home from work. Whitman sits near
the window and writes about the city he loves.
I feel the same way about it but for now can't read
his new work after running into Thoreau at the track.

He convinced me to put away my books, read less
and experience more. So I can't read Walt's poems
or travel those long lines that spread across the page
like Second and Third Avenues. I walk them now instead.

At some point I'll get us all together over drinks
and remind them I'm the kind of guy who gave up
smoking because I couldn't handle the commitment.
When everyone is more relaxed, I'll order another
round and tell them about St. Paul. I heard he fell
off his horse again, this time on a back road upstate
on his way to Kingston.

Sunday Afternoon, 1:15pm

I've been watching Peter Gunn, an old TV show
cable has been running all week. He's a private detective
in the late fifties when cars had big fins
and traffic moved like a school of sharks.
The horn section from the theme music is so powerful
construction companies in the city should use it
instead of bulldozers to knock down buildings.

During a commercial, I look out the window
over the head of my father in front of an army
barrack. It's a photo where he is shirtless
with his right hand resting on a gun in a holster
hung low around his hips. He's in the Pacific
on a tiny island whose name I can never remember
but is so long its last four letters stretch past
the shoreline and rest in the surf. He's grinning,
young and happy to still be alive. He's the man
I didn't know—looking more action hero than father.

I have a good view of the East River.
A large tanker leaves the harbor and could knock
teeth out of the river's mouth if it isn't careful.
What's left of the August heat is bent, twisted
and piled on a barge a tug pulls past two new
high rises that are the size of a center and forward
the Knicks should draft if they want to make the playoffs.

I turn the TV off and decide to go out for a walk
noticing even with a clear sky the sun isn't shining.
It means the heavy weatherman on the local news
is standing in front of a map of the U.S.—his stomach
casting a shadow over the entire East Coast.
I still get ready knowing in a couple of moments the sun
will be out again as soon as he moves back towards the Midwest.

Eating a Herd of Reindeer

My wife is in the kitchen making
holiday cookies she will place in tins
and send to family and friends.
I walk in to find her humming as she
mixes eggs, sugar and vanilla in a bowl
with a wooden spoon like the one my mother
chased me and my brothers with as kids.

I watch her fill the press with dough
thick as clay then rest the front down
against a pan and click the trigger
until there are enough wreaths to hang
on every door in the apartment building.
On top of the oven a tray of stars cools,
an entire galaxy covered in white icing.

She shifts powdered sugar over another
batch on the counter, it falls over them
like a light dusting of snow that covers
everything but the street. And I enjoy
watching her—maybe it has to do
with the way she measures things
exactly, or how I can always find
a smudge of flour on her neck and forehead.

The world I knew is the one I bolted
the door against every night when I got home.
But this is something I didn't expect, a world
that is as warm as a favorite old sweater
with holes in its elbows. And I can simply
walk into it, open a tin of reindeer cookies,
bite off an antler or two, sit down at the table,
eat a few more, then pour a large glass
of milk to help wash down the entire herd.

The City, The Snow and Two People Only

As we stroll down 3rd Avenue
it begins snowing. I point
out the first flakes are the color
of her stockings then figure
we won't have to worry if
it gets icy since her legs
have the kind of heat that can
melt anything.

We stop at the corner of 74th
so I can help her adjust her scarf.
She laughs as I make it tighter
to keep her warm the way
her arm around my waist
gets the job done for me.

On Madison we look in shop
windows, a bookstore displayed
with a new biography on the Vanderbilts
who couldn't be richer than the French
pastry in the bakery next door.

We keep walking downtown on 5th
along Central Park. She shows
me a tree with branches shaped
like fingers I admit I never noticed
or how on clear nights it holds
the moon in its hand.

On the corner of 67th I threaten
not to take another step unless
I get a kiss first. She smiles, brushes
the snow off my coat and says
she never kissed a snowman before.
I tell her I'm much too warm
to be one, then lift my collar
and button my top lump of coal.

We decide to turn back.
It's getting too cold and the snow
is already covering the city
like a white sale at Macy's.
On Lex we stop in a deli
pick up two coffees to go,
take the lids off outside
and find they forgot to add milk.

Before I take them back, enough
snowflakes have fallen in
to turn them light enough
for both of us, so we continue
uptown, sipping our coffee,
letting the snow warm our stomachs.

Butterfly

A casting director called—
told my wife, Celia, to come down
to the studio to meet him.
She was thrilled. It's an afternoon
soap that I've never watched.
I did know the woman who plays
the lead role since she is more famous
for all the Emmys she never won.
When she did win on her twentieth try,
she made the covers of all the papers;
a thin, pretty woman, who looked as flat
as Iowa holding the statue in both hands.
It was a little guy with gold wings
holding up the world, a kind of globe
with holes in it. The kind I've learned
how to live in. It reminded me
of a wiffle ball that I wanted to take outside
to hit with a bat, just to see how it feels
to knock the world around for a change.
Then my mind raced: he offers Celia
a role. In a month her fan mail piles up.
The network has no choice but to change
the title from: All My Children to All My Celia.
After her first year, her first Emmy.
She makes the covers of all the magazines,
smiling, holding it in her hand and me next to her
in a tux I bought with a bow tie resting
like a butterfly at my throat.

Shadow

When the moon is full
and can't put another thing
in its mouth, it hangs over

a tree that lost most of its leaves
to years of wind and the rest
to the latest recession.

On those nights when the sky
is clear and there are more stars
than in Hollywood, the tree's shadow

becomes just another old man,
bent, brittle and waiting
for the next bus home.

Strong Coffee

You pick up a coffee
in the diner next to
the new hardware store
celebrating its opening
with flags out front
hanging from a wire
like slices of pizza.

The coffee is strong enough
to open your eyes just in time
to notice a woman walk
past. Her legs have nothing
to do with it for a change—
it's her bulldog who looks
like Edward G. Robinson.
He almost walks into you.
As far as you can recall
it's your only brush with fame.

At the newsstand on Lex,
the paper says a king, you never
heard of before, in a country
so small it could fit with the keys
in your pocket, had died.
He ruled for as long as Elvis
was king here in the States. And
although you don't believe in guns,
you hold one in your hands
every time you rifle through
the news to get to the sports section.
Before reaching it someone
rushing by bumps into you.

It must be rush hour
as everyone hurries to the subways
and the streets put on weight
growing heavy with traffic—
a reminder how you would
like to leave the city too.
When you moved here you only
spoke English, now its your
second language.

You haven't seen a night sky
in years. When a friend said
the moon showed up the night
before and was the color
of a taxi, you can't remember
if you noticed or hailed it to take
across town. And every time
you consider moving out,
you cough, your ribs shaking
like the No. 3 bus, a reminder
that wherever the city begins
it always ends here with you.

Meteor Shower

The newspaper said there would be
a meteor shower after midnight.
Even though it rained for the past
three days the sky was clear.
You knew you'd still have to leave the city
to see much of anything. Instead
you headed over to Times Square to look
up at the neon signs since you wouldn't
need a telescope, just a piece of sidewalk.

On Twenty-Eighth and Third steam climbed
out of a manhole cover then formed
into a ghost that couldn't frighten
anyone until it thinned into a woman
you once lived with and scared you
all over again.

You stopped in a diner for a cup
of coffee and something to eat.
A waitress came over to your table
holding a bubble of coffee, poured
some into your cup and said, be careful
it's very hot. You watched her walk
away and could see by the way
she moved she knew something
about heat. So you added extra
milk and sipped. You left and didn't
finish a piece of cake that was as heavy
as the traffic going down Second.

Outside a man came up and asked if you
could spare anything to help him
out, even some change would do.

You began searching your pockets, found
nothing, then remembered the change
you had gone through during the past year.
So you dropped the last six months of it
into his paper cup, wished him luck
and walked across the street.

An Act of Seduction in the Twenty-First Century

You know as well as I
there is nothing more
than a piano between us.

So please rest your head
gently against my hip before
the moon burns a hole in my pocket.

If you close your eyes
perhaps you will see what I
did this morning at breakfast.

When I poured maple syrup
over a piece of French toast
it settled into a portrait of Christ.

Before I go any further you should
know this about me: I am
the kind of man who does not

believe in much of anything.
Now you will not be surprised
when I tell you what happened

next. I cut into it with my fork
and ate, just to feel what it is like
to chew on redemption.

A Type of Love Story

You gave up on most things
over the years until you met
a woman whose legs just wouldn't quit.
And when she slid into a pair of heels
her calves flared ever so slightly
as if to say: get down on your knees
and if you have a tongue in that mouth
of yours take it out and lick
until you are convinced this is the only
way home. And that's exactly what happened.
You got down on your knees and licked
all the words you would never use onto
her legs, a type of love story only you
would ever want to read again.

Traffic in Your Chest

Last week the sound
of a passing siren got stuck
in your throat, turned it red
and sore. Then you worried
hearing traffic in your chest
every time you coughed.
It hurt so badly, you went
to the doctor who prescribed
antibiotics that cleared it up
along with the congestion
on Fourth Street.

You are much better now—
even enjoyed the way the first
snow dusted the grass in the park,
like powdered sugar, making it
look so sweet you had to stop
in the diner across the way to order
a cup of coffee and a slice of lawn.

Walking home you almost bought
the newspaper at a stand on Fifth
until you saw the headline and lead
article about another killing
on the West Side. Even though you've
changed, it still made you
feel ashamed remembering how
for years you kept killing time
whenever you got the chance.

As you head uptown you pass
an old girlfriend's apartment building
and recall that last argument,
the one where she yelled you need
to be more open minded, flexible
and should learn to bend more.
So when change fell out of your pocket
onto the sidewalk, you wished
she had been there to watch you
bend all the way over to pick it up.
It was worth the fifty cents
just to prove her wrong.

Smoke

The guy who lives upstairs
and has never spoken to me
stops to say his mother died
last week. His eyes are wet.
He had her cremated but didn't know
where to spread her ashes since
there were a few places she loved.
He doesn't listen when I whisper
sorry. In Maine he sprinkled
just her right hand on a mountain
along with some toes, an elbow,
a bit of ear. The rest he spread over
a beach in Rhode Island until
he got down to her smile that he decided
to keep in an urn in his apartment.

I didn't want to hear anymore
about death or think about cremation.
Sorry I say to him again and that I
have to get going. On the way to the train,
I think it over, decide I will be cremated
someday too, and now would be a good time
to practice so it might not be such a shock
when the first flames reach my toes.
That night I light up an expensive cigar
to see how life can burn slowly and how my ashes
look in a tray or at least why they are worth
the smoke it takes to get there.

Crossing the River

I hail a cab that pulls over
and opens its trunk
like the mouth of a large
animal wanting to be fed.
I throw in my suitcase as if
it's a huge piece of meat,
get in the back and tell the driver
with a white cloth wrapped
around his head like vanilla custard
to take me to Kennedy Airport.
He turns onto York Avenue, still wet
and black from last night's rain.
It's the color of a cup of coffee I could use.
With a little milk and sugar,
I'd gulp down a couple of blocks
until grabbing another at the airport.
Next to me on the seat is the New York
Times. Whoever forgot it read
all the best articles and the ones he left
I didn't care about, so I folded it
and placed it back on the seat.

The driver talks into his phone
in a language filled with pebbles
and stones. We'll be at the airport
soon enough and I'm wishing
I didn't have to get on another plane.
I never liked flying or most things
that do. For years I didn't care
for the way summer flew
so I avoided July and August.
We turn onto the 59th Street Bridge
and move into a slow snake of traffic
that slides among storefronts
and brick row houses—the casual clothes
Queens wears on this side of the river.

II. Homesick

"Men travel faster now but I don't know if they go to better things."

— Willa Cather

Havana Burning

The first day on Antigua
I go into the village,
find a tobacco shop and buy
a Cuban cigar, bring it back
to the cottage I rented, then sit on
the porch to smoke it.

At home in the States I'd
be breaking the law; no wonder
for a brief moment I feel
like Humphrey Bogart as I light
up and with the cloud cover
I too am in black and white.

I know this is the closest
I'll ever get to Cuba—the entire
country rolled in my hand.
I then bite down on the shoreline,
put a match to Havana and let it burn.

To ease any guilt I feel,
I tilt my head back
against the chair and blow
smoke rings, perfect halos
a passing angel grabs
and flies to a nearby chapel
named after a wave and places it
over a statue just to make sure
it is more saint than stone.

Mango
(St. Maarten)

As soon as I walk into
the hotel room I throw my
suitcase on the bed and walk
out on to the deck to get a better
look at the ocean. Palm trees
begin to applaud, turning my face
red before the sun reaches it.
I don't know what to say
since I packed some Spanish
in with my shirts but forgot
to bring any French, so I just smile
in English and hope it will translate.

I peer over their heads at the Caribbean
and watch a surfer who looks strong
as the dollar. Another is pulled
by a parasail—a big red belly filled
with wind showing how the air has put
on some extra weight but is still
powerful and in shape. Waves crashing
along the shore break up voices
except for a nearby child's who yells
to her mother she wants a peanut butter
and jellyfish sandwich.

And I can see an island named Dog
dozing like a rock in the sun. It doesn't
stir even with gulls walking on its tail
or get up and chase a jet ski that just
passed by it. To its left, waves break
against each other forming a long white
ribbon young girls cut into strips to tie
their hair back.

A few feet away a couple of locals sit
at an open bar drinking and talking
fish. Their voices roll up and down
sounding like the Caribbean after years
of it drying in their throats. They are telling
stories of sharks that have attacked them.
I would like to join in, buy a round
and try to fit in with stories of my own
about lawyers who attacked me. For now
I'm just glad to be here for another week,
the sun already setting and the color of mango.

In the Eyes of a Dog

I am having a drink in an open bar
at a beach on St. Maarten. On the radio
Piaf is singing another Greek song,
since I don't speak a word of French.
The waitress who walks on waves
is singing with her, smiles the way
the sky does here, and places another
drink in front of me.

Over at the bar an Englishman complains
loudly how London isn't what it once was
and has changed. I want to tell him of course
it has, Dickens is dead and Churchill
is a cigar. When he gets even louder and says
something about fags to the guy mixing drinks,
I almost throw my glass at him then remember
he is only asking for cigarettes.

When I left home a close friend was still
feeling low after his wife walked out
on him six months earlier. That's why
everything on the island is so expensive.
The dollar is low too—it's just another
guy whose wife walked out a few months
ago. At least the chips are complimentary
along with the breeze coming in off the ocean.

A dog that has been roaming around
the bar stops next to my chair and stares
at me. The look in his eyes is familiar.
It's the kind of look that says I'm lost
and don't understand where I am but since
I'm standing here doesn't mean I want your scraps,
it means I made it through the day, but if
you have an easier way to get through another
I'll take it.

If the waitress didn't chase him away,
I would have told him this is how
you can at least get through another hour:
that the rocks the drinks are poured over will melt,
nothing can be built on them. So if you walk
the wooden planks on the floor to where
the sand begins and is stained white with stars,
the beach means more whenever it becomes
a piece of sky to walk home on.

Kissing the Sky

The surf along the beach
sounds like jets leaving
a runway. Surfers fly
on waves that break into
the color of cream I pour
in coffee, to make it look
as tan as my skin.

The tall men with dreadlocks,
swaying to music on the bluffs,
are palm trees and seals
sliding in on smaller more slippery
waves, become swimmers
in wet suits when they reach
the shore then get up to walk.

Salt on every breeze coming
in off the ocean is more
than I sprinkle on steak,
and the wind must have traveled
all the way from Europe,
since every gust looks French.

Here the sand is so white
the next angel I see will look
gray. And the sun setting over
the horizon is how my mother
sits on a couch, her gold dress
spreading over its cushions,
at a party that never ends
in a photo on my desk.

She said she always wanted
to move to the coast. So just
in case it is her, I pack up
my things, climb the tallest
bluff, lean my head back,
close my eyes and kiss the sky.

Basketball
        —*for Ryan*

My nephew at age six
already has a sense
of style. This morning
he put on baggy jeans,
high-top sneakers, sweatshirt
with arms tied around
his waist and a baseball
cap, its peak turned to the side
like an awning that keeps
his right ear in the shade.
I go out with him to the driveway
to shoot baskets; he says
he'll be better than Michael
Jordan the guy who plays
for the Knicks. I tell him
Jordan's with the Bulls.
He thinks it over for a few
seconds, decides I'm right,
then tries to dribble the ball.
On the second bounce
it hits his foot and rolls
down the driveway.
As he goes running after it,
I joke he dribbles better
down his chin but when
he aims for the basket,
throws the ball up and doesn't
even come close, I yell
almost try again. The ball
is stained with dirt
and water making it look
more like a globe. The smudge
near his thumb is South

America, part of his left
hand covers Europe
and when he throws it up
again it bounces back
with Russia. As I watch
him I think of the picture
my mother hung in my
bedroom when I was a kid.
It showed Christ who was just
a kid himself, holding the world
in his hands. He looked
a lot like my nephew
with the same bangs hanging
like curtains right above
his eyes. Before going to sleep
every night I wondered
what he planned doing with
the world, I even hoped
he'd toss it to me, try
something different, take
a chance, but he never did.
Instead my nephew throws
his to me; I toss it back,
because I believe in him,
saying he should give it
another shot. Most of the stains
are gone but he throws
what's left of his world
as high as he can and when
it comes down it spins
then falls through the hoop
with the sound of an angel singing.

La Jolla

The coastline here is dramatic,
like Hamlet with rock and surf.
Where I missed putting suntan
lotion on is a red patch shaped
like New York State, with Albany
resting against my ribs. I watch
surfers who keep falling off
their boards and sort of know
the feeling since, it's the kind
of ride I've been on for years
back home without the water.
Way out past them is a fishing
boat that is so distant it
reminds me of myself in my
last relationship. But life here
seems good, even the ocean
gets high on it instead of the tide.

Across the street the Valencia
Hotel with its pink paint
is much too fair for this strong
sun. They must brush it
with a coat of sunblock to keep
its stucco from burning.
And if each day begins with palm
trees on the bluffs dusting
away clouds from the sky
every morning until it shines
by 10am, then it ends here,
with me walking along the shore,
my feet wet, the air dry
as a good bottle of wine,
with Southern California melting
slowly across my shoulders.

Camden

For centuries ocean bit into
this coastline, rocks dripping
from its surf along the shore
before it left on every tide. In
town lobsters are on plates
and shirts; tourists walk on fish.
Boats leave postcards to cast
their nets, drop pots and some
carry the r's locals never use
when they talk and dump them
two miles out. In the leather shop
bags hanging on walls are faces
of fisherman sleeping on boats
anchored on canvas in the gallery
windows along Main Street.
In the park a union soldier rests
on his musket looking tired as granite
with the harbor and all his wars
behind him. On the hill the Methodist
church wears a steeple on its clock
like a wizard's hat. Every hour
its bells ring hosannas into the wings
of gulls and rattle bowls of chowder
until the next faithless man can at least
believe in cod. And at night when mist
covers the moon it's just another porch
light kept on behind a screen so whenever
you leave home you can always find
your way back again.

The Cavendish Firehouse Benefit Dance

After dinner we drove home
on the road that goes over
a mountain's foot and next
to a stream that runs even
at night. Insects bit the headlights
like snow flurries would if
August had more December in it.

We talked again about how much
we enjoyed dinner and agreed
the fish was so good it must
have loved water. She turned on
the radio to classical music,
promising to teach me more about it.
Somewhere in the middle of Bach
and Mozart was a lake she pointed
to where each winter the ice grows
thick and deep as trout. It was
the one she and her sister drove
their jeep on last January, parked
over perch and went skating.

I almost hit a dog that ran
in front of the car, but couldn't stop
the clock on the dashboard
from hitting midnight as we entered
Cavendish. We noticed a bright
light glowing from the center of town,
as if the moon had crashed,
then heard music, followed
a line of pick-up trucks parked
along the street to a banner, announcing:
The Cavendish Firehouse Benefit Dance.

It hung over a wide driveway in front
of the firehouse, with a local band
and people dancing. We both
wanted to stop for a few moments
to check things out.

An old lady who looked more
like New Hampshire than Vermont,
sat next to a five dollar donation box
and a table covered with homemade
desserts. She said the dance
and any food sold helped pay
for repairs on the firehouse. The new
wing looked to me like it was built
with concrete but she claimed
it was built with cake. We bought
coffees the color of the brownies
we decided looked so rich we couldn't
afford them, then went to sit
on a small hill next to the blacktop
to watch people dance. I held
her cup while she sat down.
Flowers grew wherever
her print dress spread over grass.

Everyone dancing were locals—
farmers dressed in jeans,
baseball caps and t-shirts with the names
of trucks and machines on them.
A large man managed a smooth
two-step with a tractor on his chest.
And we smiled at a woman who kept
spinning until she drilled a hole

in the blacktop and couldn't move.
The band took a break after a song
about a cowboy who could never
love his wife the way he loved
his horse. She then looked at her watch,
saying it was already 1:30am
and we should really get going
since Weston was still forty minutes away.

The night had cooled as we strolled
back to the car and trees began rustling
their leaves with a tune that sounded so green
I knew that even I could dance to it.

Maggots

In this high-tech age
of medical advancement
doctors have gone retro
and found maggots to clean
infected wounds with no
patient discomfort. Those
same tiny insects that look
like pedestrians moving along
the streets if you look down
from a plane. Or more like rice
when thrown outside church
at a bride and groom.

With a history of rotting
meat and horror films
where they work as extras
crawling in and out
of the eyes of a corpse,
it's difficult to accept their new
role as healers. But The New England
Journal of Medicine is pleased
with their work and hospitals have opened
maggot obedience training schools.
So after they nibble on scabs
and pus, are full on thighs or burping
up pieces of elbow, they know
enough to stop when told and never
eat towards bone.

On the Harbor

The house you rent for a week
is over one hundred years old—
its dark wood the color of clouds
with rooms in them instead of storms.
The roof and floors are crooked
but more honest than you could ever
be. It sits near the harbor's mouth
where a bridge yawns open just long
enough for a sailboat to come in
and moor a few feet from where
you are standing. The name on
its stern says Dog, no wonder it's
the kind of boat you'd rather pet
than sail.

Above you a gull hangs
like a white kite without any strings
attached before blowing over a cross
sitting on treetops. It must be
attached to a steeple trees cover
or it's actually a church founded
on maple. And with the sun so strong
the water looks dry, not as wet
as it should be but clear enough
to spot a summer school of bass
swim by.

You could stare at this harbor
and the bay beyond for as long as forever
takes until you hear the woman
you love in the shower. To get a better
look, you close your eyes as she
tilts her head back, pushing
her long brown hair away from her
face, water cascades gently
over her body, her white skin,
glistening.

Wellfleet

We find a spot we know
is far enough down the beach
when sunbathers and swimmers
become dark pieces of driftwood.
I spread my towel on the sand
like margarine and my wife
opens her umbrella until
there is a circle of shade under
it. We are near a house
hidden among the dunes—
only its roof is visible
and where it comes together
like the fingertips of a young
child praying, gulls sit.
Two snowballs that will never
melt. I look out at the ocean,
its waves are on a roll,
the kind I've been on since
April, and the sky is so clear
we can see China.

There is another house to our
left sitting on a bluff
but is far enough away
that I can rest my chin
on its roof. When I sit down,
I rub too much lotion on
my chest, causing the sun
to slide and fall into
the water, and then the sky
fades into an old bed sheet
that needs to be cleaned.
My wife begins reading articles

to me from a local paper:
how tuna like wealthy men
are a good catch; a beach in
Falmouth the ocean eats; a bake
sale in Dennis to help repair
a church steeple to go along
with its roof.

As the sky begins to clear,
everyone on the beach must
look like children from such
a distance, explaining why
the sun plays peek-a-boo with us
from behind a few leftover
clouds. I gaze out at boats
that gleam like teeth, then
towards a smile of yachts on
the horizon and begin to wonder
if we should stay here forever,
grow old the way this shoreline
does with its long white surf
before lying down again,
my eyes closed, the sand warm
against my back.

Hiking

My brother and I take a gondola
up the side of the mountain.
When the wind makes it rattle,
I feel more uneasy than Italian.
At 7000 feet we hike the rest
of the way, then take a break
when the air becomes thin as
Audrey Hepburn but with a view
more beautiful.

At the bottom of a ravine,
we notice a small lake that reflects
everything moving above it.
From where we stand it looks
like a piece of sky that fell
during last night's storm.
When an elk walks out of a clump
of trees, with antlers we could hang
our clothes on, he goes over to the water's
edge and drinks down a cloud.

The dark peaks of a mountain,
in back of a ranch with a large
herd of ants or cattle, look
like icing on top of a cake,
when baked with rock, tree and snow.
And Main Street in Steamboat Springs
is the length of a 12-inch ruler
a nun used in Math class to smack
our hands when things didn't add
up the way they should. Since
then I found most things never do.

To our south another storm
with a dark curtain of rain
hangs down on a town whose
buildings and farms are as big
as the periods I used on the postcards
I sent home. It won't reach us
for another hour, enough time to
get back.

We decide to take another path
down, with the rest of the valley
stretched out before us, a green
rug our mother would never
have let us walk on with our shoes.

House of Books

I knew I had spent
too much time in the city
when I drove past a herd
of steaks and leather coats
instead of cows. I was on
my way to a friend's house
in Connecticut who wanted
me to stay there while she
was away on business.

The original house was built
in 1810 in between birches
and maples, the rest was added
on between wars. The Berkshires
were spread across a large picture
window in the living room.
I could make out a white house
the size of the top button I lost
on my shirt and might take
it to sew on before leaving.
It should be more comfortable
with a home resting against
my neck.

Books lined the walls
with enough stories to build
a high rise taller than any
on Fifth Avenue. I helped
myself to a few, sat down
in a chair next to a portrait
of a nineteenth century land
owner whose face was shaped
like a cathedral and opened
Ship of Fools. I was relieved
to find it wasn't about my relatives
sailing on Long Island Sound.

Then I spent some time
with The Birds of North America
and later, except for the names,
found nothing new in New American
Writing, so I opened The Collected
Poems of W.B. Yeats and to poems
that are new every time I read them.

It was getting dark; I took a break,
got up to turn on some lights and gazed out
at the garden. It looked English
and much too beautiful to be left
out for the night. If I had help,
I would have brought it in
until morning then went over
to light a fire.

As the wood sparked and began
to roar the way the roses did
in the garden, I spotted a copy
of Profiles in Courage and was soon
convinced that if JFK knew about
the last woman I lived with,
he would have made me the last chapter.
Later I found large picture books,
lay down on my back and traveled
by couch to Colorado, France and Greece.
All in just under three hours.

Tequila

The surf pounds the shoreline
the way your heart does against
your chest after a jog, convincing
you these waves run instead of roll
all the way from Europe. Everyone
seems to end up here; you've met
Germans, French and Asians. Cubans
are cigars. The small place you rented
is just south of San Jose near a bluff
where a cactus stands with its arms up
as if it is being robbed. Every time
you come home the dog next door
growls in Spanish then barks in English
when you don't turn around to leave.

You are learning to love the food
here and to make some Mexican dishes
yourself, but since you found out
what it feels like to broil in this heat
you stick to grilling everything.
During the first few weeks after
getting settled, you enjoyed watching
the surfers on Zipper's Beach until
they reminded you how your boss
rode you about anything that went
wrong. He didn't realize you knew how
to quit better than anyone on the job,
then rode the next bus out of town.

Just last week you knew you
still had it in the cantina a few
rocks down from your place when
you told the waitress you saw the name
in rhinestones over her breast
pocket in the stars the night before.
After she half smiled and put
another tequila under your chin,
she walked away, shook her head
and muttered gringos. Then you headed
home, got into bed, turned on the ceiling
fan that spun a breeze as you wrapped
the sheet around you like a tortilla
and fell asleep.

Baja

On the map the Baja Peninsula
looks like a horse's leg; you are
renting a small apartment near
the hoof in San Jose. There's a mountain
in the window whose peak is shaped
like the Parthenon overlooking the Sea
of Cortez that sits in for the Aegean.
Large waves keep rolling in; they seem
furious at the beaches for making
them end in surf, so they crash
and spit foam. You have never seen
anger like this before, the kind
where there is so much wet behind it.

The men here stare, whistle and hit
on every woman who looks or may be
a tourist. Even the stars wink at
the coastline that has real curves
or must look full figured from the sky.
And there are thousands of stars.
Every evening you can find the Big
Dipper hanging over your head.

In Old Town you noticed a small
kidney shaped pool in back
of a house that was boarded up. You
regret no longer speaking to a friend
at home who is on dialysis, needs
a transplant and is waiting
for a donor. You almost call
to tell him about it then decide
not to since he'd only yell
his illness is none of your business
anymore and besides the chlorine
has to be a perfect match.

You have already fallen into
a routine here. Every morning
you get coffee going, roll eggs
in a flour tortilla the way you
never could roll a joint. The days
are long with an hour or two
left over you just don't need, so
you trim, filet and feed them
to the skinny mutt who followed
you home and never left. And
you have decided to stay longer
than planned since the sun is just
the way you like it: hot and not too
spicy.

Near the Lake

Elvis was king that summer
and the fins on my father's car
made me think fish. The house
we rented was built near the lake
after the war. In the backyard,
my younger brother and I put mud
on stones until the sun baked them
cake, ate with our mouths closed
then faked ourselves full. We shot
birds with sticks, found gold in dirt
and bought France for ten rocks.

When the girl from across
the street came to play we taunted
her face red, stopped tears
with apologies then dared her pants
down to prove she could never
be like us. By July she promised
to marry me if I took her fishing
over the valley that was once
filled with farms before the county
flooded it into a lake. So we
rowed with her to where the water
was deep as a barn, then dropped
her line with ours into a corral of perch.

Every Friday night I waited
for my father to arrive from the city
but always fell asleep in the middle
of crickets. The next morning leaves woke
me rustling songs the air made crisp
and I smelled the coffee I wasn't
allowed to drink for another seven years.
At breakfast my father first told
us about growing up near Dublin,
his mother dying when he was my age
and a father who kept losing jobs
every time he drank himself boss.

One Sunday over breakfast
my father told us stories
about coming to the United States
and the Depression. I wondered
if times were really harder
than Math class, then stuck
my knife into the eyes
of eggs, wishing mine were
the color of yolks. Later
we went to church where our hymns
cleaned air of sin and sermons scared
me saint.

My brother and I let August
turn our skin the only
kind of pink guys could wear,
built a fort in a tree
that convinced us our father
was stronger than anything oak
and found a dog we could never
bring home. We walked roads
that were pebble and dirt,
followed a path in the woods
and discovered a pond we knew
no man had ever seen.

One night I snuck out alone
and walked paths lit by moon
back to the pond. A deer drank from it,
stopped after spotting me, then hid
among pine. I stared down at the water
and my face floating among stars.
Then dropped a rock into my forehead.
As my face broke and floated away
a croak that didn't sound like a frog spooked
me home. Jumping under the covers,
I tried to sleep with the sound
of twigs still cracking in my ears,
my hands shaking with trees.

The boy from up the street
who kept losing his glasses,
then his teeth, told us about a house
that sat on treetops. Later we found
it was on a hill and the old man
who lived in it killed kittens from each
litter he couldn't give away.
We once saw him putting a sack
in the engine of his Ford
then he turned on the ignition
and let it hum until his car ran out of cats.

The summer ended with my father sitting
on the porch drinking a glass of wine
and my mother in the kitchen
at the stove raising the flame under a pot,
singing a Doris Day song I can no longer hear.

Capri

We take the ferry to Capri
from the dock at Positano.
There isn't a cloud in the sky,
that is clear as English, as we
head up the Amalfi Coast.
The mountains remind me
of my father napping after
a large dinner. I can make
out cars shining in the glare
as they move along the cliff
road that is thin as pasta
and for the first time ever
a bus becomes a gleam in my eye.

Twenty minutes later we can
spot Sorrento that is now
a porcelain dish shattered against
stone and as the waves rock and roll
like Chuck Berry; a seasick young
woman the size of a small village
outside Salerno is helped down
from the top deck. I know little
Italian but the look on her face
is easy to translate. It takes
four crew members to help her
on the steps and over to the railing.
And then there is Capri: rising up
out of the water along with something
else to shake my beliefs. Perhaps
there is a God—who else could
have dropped those rocks into
the Sea of Naples just for the hell of it.

The ferry pulls into Marina Grande.
It's filled with shops, cafes,
tourists and boats with names
like the dinners on the menu
in the little Italian joint back home
on 1st. We stop in the Café Augusto
for a cup of espresso with a smile
of lemon floating in it, pay
with Monopoly money then decide
to take an open-roofed bathtub taxi
since we only have a few hours
until the next ferry. We take
a road up a hill that is long
as a novel to the Villa Jovis
where Tiberious held court,
and where goats have ruled since
45 A.D. and then to the Salto
di Tiberio, a cliff, where he pitched
villagers into the sea since
soccer wouldn't be invented
for another thousand years.

We meet a local who speaks
to us in broken English—most
words fall out of his mouth
in pieces that could never be
glued back together. He tells us
we need a wick not just a day
to see Capri, how he loves basketabowl,
The New Yucka Nooks and that once
he spent two wicks in the downatone
zone of Manhattana. He shows
us a short cut to take on foot,
rather than take a cab, since we
can see more that way.

We follow his route, stop
in the Gardens of Augustus
just to let our eyes fill with cliffs,
sky and water. Waves roll
like vowels in the mouths of two
old men arguing over wine
outside a café along the Via Camerelle.
The water looks green, young
but gives away its real age
when it reaches the shore, exposing
its white beard of surf. So we
decide to hurry down and catch
the next ferry before the Sea of Naples
becomes too old to carry one more
boat back to Positano.

Homesick
    (Athens)

The Greek Orthodox Cathedral
in Plaka reminds me of home
every time its bells ring
since there is so much Methodist
in their echo. And the ruins
that are fenced off to keep tourists
out, can't keep comparisons
away to my Uncle Seamus
who looked the same after
his third wife walked out on him.
English breaks in the mouths
of locals like the family who runs
the Athenian Diner around the block
from my apartment back home.
And I can't help walking into
a taverna after seeing its New York
Pizza sign. I order a slice that looks
more like Miami than Manhattan
and when the waitress asks if
there is anything else she can get
me, I ask for a soda and the score
of last night's Yankee game.

About the Author

Kevin Pilkington's poetry collection, *Spare Change* won the La Jolla Poets Press National Book Award, *Ready to Eat the Sky* was published by River City Press which was a finalist for an Independent Publishers Books Award and his chapbook, *Getting By*, was awarded the Ledge Poetry Prize. His poems have appeared in many anthologies including *Birthday Poems: A Celebration, Western Wind, Contemporary Poetry of New England* and a wide variety of journals, including: *The New York Quarterly, Poetry, Ploughshares, Iowa Review, Boston Review, Yankee, Columbia, Greensboro Review,* and *The Valparaiso Review.* A four-time Pushcart Prize nominee, he is a member of the full-time writing faculty at Sarah Lawrence College and teaches a workshop in the graduate program at Manhattanville College.

About NYQ Books™

NYQ Books™ was established in 2009 as an imprint of The New York Quarterly Foundation, Inc. Its mission is to augment the *New York Quarterly* poetry magazine by providing an additional venue for poets already published in the magazine. A lifelong dream of NYQ's founding editor, William Packard, NYQ Books™ has been made possible by both growing foundation support and new technology that was not available during William Packard's lifetime. We are proud to present these books to you and hope that you will continue to support The New York Quarterly Foundation, Inc. and our poets and that you will enjoy these other titles from NYQ Books™:

Amanda J. Bradley	*Hints and Allegations*
Joanna Crispi	*Soldier in the Grass*
Ira Joe Fisher	*Songs from an Earlier Century*
Ted Jonathan	*Bones and Jokes*
Fred Yannantuono	*A Boilermaker for the Lady*

Please visit our website for these and other titles:

www.nyqbooks.org

www.ingramcontent.com/pod-product-compliance
Lightning Source LLC
LaVergne TN
LVHW011429080426
835512LV00005B/346